The New Bold Standard

THE NEW BOLD STANDARD

*How Adding Specialized Of Counsel Attorneys
Can Transform Your Law Firm*

J.D. HOUVENER

Sponsor: Bold IP, PLLC - 800-849-1913 - www.boldip.com

© 2017 J.D. Houvener
All rights reserved.

ISBN: 1978143338
ISBN 13: 9781978143333

Intro

The internet has changed the way we do things, both dramatically and permanently. It has forced almost every professional field to totally reorganize its approach to marketing and managing its services—and the legal field is no exception.

With an online presence, such as a website or social media account, the ability to accept digital payments, and a greater availability of information, lawyers and law firms alike are able to reach more potential clients than ever before.

Back when I first chose to practice law, the goal I set for myself was to be at the top of a "megafirm." My vision was to offer multiple top-notch services from engaged, ethical attorneys to a variety of clients.

Now that the landscape is shifting, I have discovered that there is a new, more efficient way to achieve the same results: the "Of Counsel" relationship.

Chapter 1

A Closer Look

The Goals

Though the business structure may be different than that of a traditional brick and mortar firm, the same goals I had for a large, integrated firm can still be reached with an Of Counsel partnership.

My four main goals are to:

1. **Diversify Revenue Streams**
2. **Serve the Legal System**
3. **Promote Innovation & Business**
4. **Engage in Collective Learning**

Internet access has increased the exposure of, and so the demand for, attorneys. It has also widened the pool of prospective clients. This has come to mean that more attorneys are now able to work for themselves from home, or start their own small firms.

Because these scaled-down firms can handle only so many clients, their best success comes from focusing on a niche. That's why one of the biggest areas of growth in the legal field today is in specializations.

But that doesn't mean that general practice or business firms can't share in this growth! The surge in specializations can also help general or business practice firms earn MORE money AND more clients!

This has been proven by my own entrepreneurial journey with my patent firm, BOLD Intellectual Property Law —and I want to show you how. Not only am I going to give you the benefit of my experience by naming best practices, I'll give you tips on how to get started and leave you with a clear path to success!

The current concept and practice of the of counsel relationship is the basis for the process that I have used to successfully promote and grow my firm through partnerships with other law firms and attorneys.

My first step has always been to approach principle partners and explain the clear advantages of partnering with a specialty firm. In this book, I'll explain these benefits in the context of our 4 Main Goals.

Goal 1: Diversify Revenue Streams

One way to do this is to expand your services. Prior to engaging of counsel, a would-be Host firm is not able to offer, for example, patent application filing services for an existing client.

Why does this matter? We will discuss this at length in later sections, but for now I'll give you a quick overview.

Perhaps a client has entrusted your firm with the entity formation for their new business. It may be the case that this new business is built around a new invention. Unfortunately for your firm, because business or general practice attorneys do not take the patent bar, they must refer this client out to another firm. This scenario is less than ideal (to say the least) for both the client and the referring firm. Not only does the firm miss an opportunity for more business, they may be forced to refer their client to a firm they are unfamiliar with—leaving them vulnerable to the unvetted.

Referrals vs. Relationships

Cultivating a relationship with a patent firm allows you to advertise these additional, specialized services and becomes, essentially, an extension of your firm itself. The Of counsel patent firm is an independent contractor, or rather, an employee or member of the Host firm—and that's just how they should be introduced to both potential and current clients. This way, your clients have confidence that their patent attorney is in congruency with the level of service that you maintain.

This also opens up the potential for clients that general practice or business firms may not have previously been able to take on. For example, your business or general law firm wants to work with startups, developing businesses or even mature businesses looking to sell, right? Well, many of these clients will inevitably come across patent law issues.

But without passing that patent bar, your firm is unable to handle any problems regarding this subject matter. Even if the client is primarily a business client, if the business is based upon a new technology, patenting this technology is often times the first or primary legal issue that needs to be dealt with. Don't lose that client to other firms because you can't deliver what they need—you can!

Conversely, if a potential of counsel client has technology that needs patent law protection, they will likely also need help with a business entity formation, operating agreement, employment agreement, vendor sales agreements and so forth—all of which you, as a "Host" law firm, could very happily to take on for your new client.

The other part of this win-win is something I will go over in more detail in the next section. I'm taking about the immediate benefit of maintaining of counsel relationships! Because as the Host firm you bear the administrative burden of handling the client's file, you get compensated with an agreed-upon percentage of the patent billables (that is, patent billables or billables for whichever specialty you may choose to offer).

Goal 2: Serve the Legal System

Of course, this arrangement is not just about money; it's about being able to serve the client more wholly and efficiently through your firm. Indeed, the idea behind the of counsel relationship is that <u>your firm</u> is the client's exclusive source for their legal needs.

Again, because of the patent bar requirement, without a close relationship with a qualified patent agent it might be necessary for a general practice or business law firm to simply refer out cases like the ones I described earlier. More often than not, unfortunately, these referrals are very informal and the referring firm can never be certain that their client will get the best possible legal support. Can you imagine how that might affect your firm's reputation and therefore its bottom line?

Goal 3: Promote Innovation & Business

Because many specialty practice areas, especially patent law, are so closely interwoven with a lot of other legal issues (such as invention assignment agreements, employment agreements, trademark law or trade secret law issues, licensing agreements and so on) a host firm is in a position to readily provide any of these non-specialized services all while being able to manage their client's experience with the specialty firm.

Now, without a smooth transition and clear communication between the host and the specialty firm, think how often the issues above could be overlooked or never even addressed. Rather than view the client's case, or their invention and the business formation that supports the monetization of that new technology, as parts of a bigger picture, the process is compartmentalized in this scenario. From my perspective, this causes business on all sides to suffer. We miss our best opportunities to be forward thinking. Instead of advising the client on how to be proactive and best leverage their intellectual property assets, we have to spend that time playing catch up with them.

But what about _your_ business? With a patent attorney on your team, your firm now has access to a client base of inventors, including garage inventors even, who are starting businesses as well as growing and medium sized innovation companies. These entrepreneurs and organizations are _all_ going to need representation at some point!

For one, these companies have ongoing research and development. They will inevitably need the support of a general practice firm because they are not yet big enough to have dedicated, full-time general counsel. General or business law firms (like yours) that have dedicated relationships with specialized attorney firms are especially attractive to these start-up sized, small and medium companies because <u>you</u> can now take on their cases with the confidence to:

- Resolve the entire matter for your client—not just the merger and acquisition, but maybe even the evaluation of the Intellectual Property (IP);
- Create strategies to license your client's IP;
- Negotiate the best results for your client, knowing that you have a team of specialists backing you.

GOAL 4: COLLECTIVE LEARNING

Your of counsel team will also be a source of new information; a teacher of the best practices that they have cultivated, or perhaps methods they have learned from other host firms they may work with.

Collective learning and legal synergy improve the quality of our field and the vitality of our own businesses. Beyond simple best practices, of counsel partnerships can also benefit your firm by introducing patentable systems and processes that are used by other business and general practice law firms; bringing attention and understanding to possible weakness in firm management; and thereby, equipping you with better tools to articulate value propositions for yourself as well as for your clients.

Of counsel relationships can help connect you to potential clients in a number of exciting, thriving fields. The best way to start the search for possible Of counsel candidates is to ask yourself: what interests me?

Below is a short list of popular specialists that can greatly benefit your general practice, business law, immigration or trademark law firm:

- Tax Specialists
- M&A Specialists
- Bankruptcy
- Family Law
- Trusts and Estate Planning

Notes

Chapter 2

Best Practices

In order for your new business venture to thrive, there are a number of best practices that I recommend you follow to establish and maintain a successful of counsel relationship. These practices are drawn from my own real-world experience and based on focused action.

In this useful section, I have highlighted some of the best methods in every aspect of the partnership from philosophy to finances. What follows is the backbone of a code that I believe to be crucial for success. Use it as a foundation to create your own.

Before You Sign

Because my firm has been contracted as of counsel for many patent cases, I know what information and considerations these firms should provide you with. Before you sign, be sure who you partner with is willing and able to do the job right.

TRUST YOUR OF COUNSEL FIRM

In order to forge a successful relationship with an of counsel firm, you need to have confidence in their expertise. To do that, make sure you get "trained" in your firms new practice area. Ask them to go over the following:

1. **Get an overview of the specialty** practice area, as well as any information on regional laws that can affect your particular case or client.
2. **A thorough review of any linked or related services that you, as the host firm, can offer** a new specialty area client. This is important because there are a lot of opportunities or issues that may be overlooked simply because the connections are not obvious.

For example, let's say your firm was managing a divorce case. Now, if you wouldn't necessarily think to call your Of counsel IP attorney to advise you on this matter, you may want to reconsider. I say this because, by nature of a divorce case, assets are being accounted for. Perhaps the husband and wife were co-owners of a business. Certainly that business will have IP assets. A patent attorney can expertly separate, value and even identify unrecognized assets.

Work With "One-Layer" Firms

What do I mean by "one layer"? Well, the of counsel law firm you partner with should be comprised of a dedicated group of attorneys that will represent you client themselves in the specialty practice areas. In other words, they should not be sub-contracting your of counsel—they should have specialized attorneys on staff.

Generally speaking, I say this because it is important to maintain a camaraderie; a unified, planned and directed system. This is what will allow you to be the most efficient and deliver "one voice" to the client. Contracting a two-layer (or more) of counsel agreement leaves the partnership susceptible to the pitfalls of a "too many cooks" scenario.

Like I said, both firms need to uphold a dedicated cohesiveness that will engender the growth of your brand and the growth of the specialty practice within that brand. Typically, sub-contractors of of counsel firms aren't going to be as committed to your client as a partner that works directly with you. Perhaps they have other commitments, other jobs, or even conflicts with your of counsel firm. These cracks are going to show through in the quality and overall service level to you and, in the end, to the client.

In addition, more than "one-layer" agreements increase your liability by creating additional areas of scrutiny for ethical conflict. If the of counsel firm is comprised of contract attorneys, it does not enable the recognition of one brand, of one firm. Instead, it's a collection of five or six or seven different attorneys, and they're all operating as individuals--suddenly the host firm can no longer depend on who (or what firm) their representation will come from. Consistency, crucial to reaching and maintaining our goals, is lost.

Bottom line: a group of contractors is difficult to manage. They are serving more than one host law firm at a time **indirectly**, with more than one attorney serving one host law firm. Without an employee-based of counsel firm, any systems, methods or procedures that were successful in the past, or could work for you in the future are not going to have the same effectiveness, level of commitment, dedication or teamwork.

Roles, Relationships And Communication

Ok, so you've vetted and partnered with a specialty firm that you know will take good care of your clients and have begun marketing your new services (more on this in future sections). You are finally ready to take advantage of the benefits of your of counsel relationship. Now, you want to be prepared for the first steps.

There are generally **two initial scenarios** with a potential case: the shared client is a prospective or brand new; or, you are contracting services for an existing client.

While the first steps in this shared relationship may be easiest with an existing client, they are no less important. Remember, clear communication of roles is crucial to the success of this triple venture.

Here's what I suggest:

Considered, Structured Introductions

For a first meeting, the host firm should schedule a phone conference, video conference or, if possible, an in-person meeting with their client and their of counsel attorney. The handoff is most comfortable in this way, as the client gets the sense that they are simply meeting with another attorney from your (host) firm.

Truly, this is the intention: for the of counsel attorney or attorneys to perform just as their host firm would. This leads in to my next point about who gets administrative priority.

Prioritizing The Host Firm

The of counsel relationship is one that needs to balance several factors in order to work as flawlessly as possible. The most important of these factors is for both host and of counsel to understand that the client "belongs" to the host firm—not the of counsel firm. That means that the qualifications and criteria of the Host firm should be prioritized.

That said, even if the client appears to be a perfect fit for the of counsel firm, if this is not the case for the host firm, the arrangement may not be in anyone's the best interest. Remember, in the end, the host firm is the one to manage the relationship with the client, including billing, administration, client-facing policies and invoicing.

And as I have already emphasized, the client who is a best match will have at least <u>some</u> potential to garner business for the host firm itself—not just the of counsel. Stay cognizant of the fact that any potential crossover business may not always be apparent, but the client's future needs should always be anticipated and addressed. As with a patent law arrangement, to use our ongoing example, the host firm should recommend to the client services such as entity formation or the creation of membership or operating agreements, etc. even if the first step is to help them work through a patentability search or patent application process.

Listen To Your Clients

Paying attention to your client and anticipating their needs is a great way to not only create potential business for your firm and better help your client, but also to fully take advantage of your of counsel partner relationship.

How?

Let's say that your client is a woman in her forties seeking a divorce attorney. She is in a middle income bracket, but has acquired some assets.

While it is typical to ask such a client about her job and/or income, truly listening and considering her answer offers you a unique opportunity to discover new ways to serve her needs and create revenue for yourself and your of counsel.

To illustrate my point: perhaps she responds to the question of what she does for work by telling you that she is a teacher, but she also does artwork on the side. A lot of attorneys would probably gloss over the second part in an instance like this—doing at most a simple accounting of any income generated from selling this artwork. But buy listening and asking further questions, you can determine what, if any, other legal issues she may be overlooking. In this case, perhaps trademarking a brand or image, or even copyright protection.

Becoming engaged allows you to serve individuals on a higher level, facilitating more money making potential for everyone involved. In fact, this simple act is so powerful, it encompasses all four of our main goals!

Upfront, Flat-Fee Billing

The 80-20 Split

Now the process is in motion. As the host firm, you are responsible for managing client information, documents and scheduling. The of counsel firm solely performs the services of their legal specialty.

Part of the emphasis on clarity that I have been stressing throughout this book includes straightforward billing agreements. This is made easy by employing a simple 80/20 flat rate split.

Of course, it is ultimately up to the two negotiating firms to come to an understanding on how exactly, or to what degree, the 80-20 split is appropriate.

For example, say I file a provisional patent application for the client of a host firm. The client is charged a fee and my firm takes 80 percent while my host firm gets their agreed-upon 20 percent. Now, once I file the provisional application, I have to then file a follow-up, non-provisional application within one year. You and your of counsel would have to decide if, in a case like this, the host firm should retain another 20 percent for the second milestone, or if the initial 20 percent includes any administrative follow up.

While a general 80/20 split is best practice, there is no one way to manage details like mandatory follow up milestones. I recommend anticipating the fact that there will inevitably be special circumstances that will need to be discussed and decided.

About Other Billing Methods

Hourly fees can be troublesome, especially when billing of counsel clients. Payment plans are high risk: oftentimes, client finances come and go. There are several reasons why I suggest charging flat fees that are due upfront:

a. **Accuracy in Quoting**. Once your of counsel firm teaches you more about how their specialty works, your firm will most likely end up being able to describe and then quote fees for these different types of specialty services for current or potential new clients. Flat fee structures allow for simple, efficient quoting with a transparency that your client will love.
b. **Accuracy in Billing**. With an hourly arrangement, there are a lot of channels that the billing information needs to pass through before the client actually gets billed. The attorney of counsel firm needs to

send the hours to the principal, which would then of course be sent to their billing department. Once the invoice was sent to you, the host firm, then the invoice would have to get sent to <u>your</u> billing department. That's at least four steps before the bill even reaches the client. The risk of errors is way too high with this many hand-offs.

c. **Getting Paid**. Charging a flat fee—due in full <u>before</u> work begins—ensures that your entire team gets paid. This also means that the attorney of record has the resources to perform their job to the best of their ability.

Invoicing

a. Host collects all fees up front. Of counsel bills the host firm once work is completed.
b. Client pays 100% to of Counsel, who then sends 20 percent to host. This method should only be used when specifically required by the law or as a stipulation of a malpractice insurance policy.

General Pricing

a. **Commensurate Value**. Of counsel should price services for host firms exactly the same way they price service at their home firm. That means same services at the same price points. In other words, a client sourced through a host should receive the exact same value as one represented solely by the of counsel.

Keep Compliant

Get Malpractice Insurance

While it may not be a legal requirement for your particular firm, to work with an independent contractor you <u>must</u> have malpractice coverage. I have experienced great successes providing of counsel work—but it is common for plans to go awry and the need to protect yourself and your firm goes without saying.

Now, if you already carry malpractice insurance, then you will have to check to see if independent contractors are covered under your rider. If there is no such provision in your rider or policy and you are required to rewrite or extend coverage to include independent contractors, then any concomitant increase in cost should be shared by the two firms. I typically propose a 50/50 split of the upgraded premium, or a percentage of an existing premium that covers the hiring of independent contractors.

At the end of the day, however, regardless of <u>how</u> your carrier manages your coverage, it is imperative that the client be absolutely clear on which attorney is performing what work to help support any legal decisions made on the malpractice insurance protection. This information can all be easily spelled out in the engagement letter from the host law firm.

Cross Your T's, Dot Your I's

Being organized and scrupulous with filings, documentation, contracts and communication lays the foundation for a smooth, effective and efficient work experience. This leads to more and more revenue! But remember, your ducks <u>need</u> to be in a row:

1. Get **malpractice insurance.**
2. Make sure that you and your of counsel **operate from a place of ethics**. Then, educate your client on these ethics, both in general law and for the specialty. More than one agenda will confuse, hinder and ultimately sour any kind of contracted working relationship.
3. **Clarify for the client**—officially in the engagement letter and then again at every milestone—who represents them in each subsequent matter of representation. Keep in mind that numbers two and three on this mini list are ongoing. As with any legal matter or business proceeding, you must be vigilant every step of the way.

Build Networks

Re-Invest In Each Other

Work as one.

Just as a Host firm keeps an ear to the ground for clients that may need the help of a specialty attorney, so the of counsel firm should foresee and prepare for the ancillary needs that go with having IP to protect. This policy of referring back becomes a reciprocally beneficial relationship that can help both of your firms thrive.

Acting and functioning like one firm gains client trust and increases client confidence—now they feel comfortable tackling that operating agreement, or even give their colleagues your number!

Learn and Improve the Legal System

I think we can all agree that the legal system is a body of knowledge that can constantly be improved upon. It is by no means a perfect system—but we <u>can</u> do our own part to contribute to that improvement. And it all adds up.

Keeping one another accountable in regards to high standards makes attaining a service and legal congruency easier. We work to obtain a practical synergy that streamlines communication and, in this way, cumulatively raises the quality of legal services across firms.

Of course, higher standards for case management are not the only way to enhance the legal system. We must also **learn from and support one another**.

Once you begin working with other attorneys in your new practice areas, you will learn how issues in these cases relate to legal matters that scope beyond the specialty. Soon, you will be able to recognize and respond to possible issues in real time—servicing the client that much better! Not to mention the boost in your billables!

Support and Branch Out

Again, one of—if not the greatest—aspects of counsel partnerships is the ability **to diversify revenue streams** by building alliances. Once you have fully integrated patent and IP law services into your firm, you can branch out into other specialty areas (or vice versa); immigration or estate law, for example.

As your client base continues to grow, you may find yourself calling upon your of counsel(s) more frequently. A steady flow of work, if you have a chosen a solid firm to do business with, engenders enthusiasm and creates momentum. This momentum, if translated into action on behalf of your firms, generates both revenue and important, perhaps crucial, opportunities for (ethical) legal innovation. If on behalf of the client, will lead to ways in which we, as attorneys, can better equip the individual to gain control over their personal lives, finances, creations and innovations.

Notes

Chapter 3

Get Started

Bringing It All Together

When

Now that we've gone through the "What" about the rewards of healthy of counsel relationships and "How" you can work with these attorney firms to reach mutual goals, it's time to talk about how to get started finding a partner.

Who

This path takes a partner who values transparency; a firm committed to positive growth.

Successful partnerships are always win-win situations

But what makes them successful? Particularly, what agreements are made to ensure everyone gets what they need to take care of the client?

We discussed best practices in roles and relationships in terms of client perception, but in order to get the most out of this venture, we need to take a deeper look at our attitudes about the relationship between the two firms.

What guiding principles do we use when we are interacting with another entity that is also an extension of ourselves?

1. **Understand Long-Term Goals.** The communication of, and accounting for, one another's long-term goals leads to greater clarity of purpose and mutual value.
2. **Unify Forces.** Rather than use cutthroat tactics to scoop clients and dominate competition, do business in a way that supports growth (i.e. makes more revenue) by unifying forces with other firms.
3. **Genuine Expertise.** It is imperative that you are satisfied with his or her expertise. Be mindful of the language in their offer: it should reflect an awareness of _your_ long-term goals, a willingness to work with your administrative policies and a **clear core level of competency**

in that specialty. Verify that the attorneys you consider are fully capable of handling nearly any situation that comes under the umbrella of their specialty.

Once you decide that you want to grow your firm, it will be your responsibility to do some self-analysis and to create a profile and a process for interviewing and negotiating offers from proposing offices.

Where

Start Locally

Whether you choose to work with a solo practitioner, a small practice with a handful of attorneys, or even a bigger law firm of 20 or 30+ attorneys, the ability to connect with a potential partner face to face is the best way to establish the level of trust that is necessary to build the foundation for the most successful partnerships between host and of counsel.

I recommend seeking new partnerships with **local attorneys** especially if this is your first time reaching out to another firm.

So, where can you find out who's out there?

There are two main ways to identify your potential colleagues:

1. **Ask other colleagues.** Get a referral from your law school associates or from the state, local, or county bar association who may be part of, or who works closely with, a general or business practice firm.
2. **Online Research.**
   a. **LinkedIn**. While I maintain that local partnerships are best, as of the writing of this book, LinkedIn remains the premier professional networking internet website, where an extensive database of individual professionals and businesses can connect with those that they may not otherwise have been able to contact.
   b. **Other, Local Networking Sites.**
      i. Townsquared
      ii. Local Growth
      iii. eLocal

The most important question to ask yourself is whether or not your of counsel has the right characteristics to help you meet your long-term goals of growing revenue and finding new and better ways to service clients.

Maintain Perspective and Manage Expectations

Essentially, the approach to of counsel that works will be any one that prioritizes the relationship and is in touch with the entrepreneurial spirit.

As a host firm, you will need to welcome a new way of practicing law. If you've read this far and are still considering my suggestions for of counsel, than you are presumably comfortable viewing a law practice as a business rather than solely a trade or profession in the traditional sense.

Why

Yes, Making Money is Important. It's Just Not the Entire Point.

Of course making money is a key consideration. My point is that we can do it while serving the law and the citizen.

Why does our attitude matter? Overly-aggressive and competitive methods of gaining clients tend to weaken the law and the all-around quality of service by limiting access to knowledge. Certainly some fields claim to thrive on such a culture. The legal field, however, is not one.

In other words, the ways in which we make money are more important than making money itself. My proposed business model is a transition away from secrecy, from a hold-on-to-mine-try-and-take-yours mentality and a shift into a let's-share-and-succeed-together-because-there's-no-reason-not-to attitude.

Being able to serve clients more efficiently than ever before generates more need for law services. Accordingly, it should come as no surprise that this means there will be more business for the firms and greater progress for the client.

It soon starts to become obvious: the best successes come from unifying our collective forces.

We put feathers in the respective caps of progress and innovation

Does that claim sound a bit theatrical? Perhaps to some. But real progress is built on trust and hard work.

Many times, local companies looking for IP attorneys have been formed to be a vehicle for bringing some type of patented product or intellectual property to the marketplace. Whether it be some type of tool or engine, a film or a writing, or maybe even a website with proprietary content, the host law firm who can help serve them in a multitude of facets, will now have exposure to this professional and a chance to make them a client.

In many cases, this said business may even be unaware of the services they might already need. For example, maybe they're out of compliance with regulations for their goods or services, maybe their contracts are aging or maybe they don't even have contracts!

This kind of business or start up exemplifies the perfect opportunity for an of counsel lawyer (in this case patent law) to bring in new clients for you both and how your firms can work in concert to deepen the relationship with all clients.

Getting the Word Out

Make a Formal Announcement

The media and the press are powerful tools for announcing your new partnership. I believe of counsel relationships with host law firms should be touted. These partnerships should be shared with as many people as possible—both within (including the contact lists of both law firms), and outside of, the legal community.

When two law firms make a commitment to enhance the field and the client experience, it is something to celebrate because the only agenda is the betterment of each party. This path is always an all-around win.

As the host law firm, you should take the lead in publicizing the new alliance. **Make an official announcement** via press release, on social media, to your email and snail-mail lists, your blog or any other marketing or media platforms you may use. Introduce your firm's latest exciting development: you now also handle specialty legal matters. The superior legal services your general or business practice is known for now has a new cutting edge **value proposition**: the expert research, care and results your clients receive can now be reviewed by attorneys who are uniquely licensed in a specialized area of legal knowledge.

Be effusive, promote with confidence.

This announcement will set the tone for building a rapport between your existing clients and your new partners. You are introducing the next evolution in your business and you only get one first impression.

Likewise, the of counsel firm should advertise their relationship with you to <u>their</u> community. This includes both their internal clients and any other firms they are of counsel to. In this way, the potential for a larger, more unified network has again increased.

On that note, I'd like to point out here that in **no way** is the relationship between the of counsel and another host law firm harmed by a separate relationship with another host law firm—so as long as they have the resources to support it. On the contrary, benefits increase **in every way.** Both firms get clients and clients get increasingly better legal help.

Announcement Checklist

1. **Choose Your Platforms.** Think of every outlet you can use. Bear in mind that different types of media require different types of marketing.
2. **Gather Your Contacts.** This is the time to clean current lists and/or buy new lists. Also, just like with different media, mind your audience. You may not want to present your new partnership to existing clients the same way as potential clients or as you would to other law firms, for example.
3. **Create your Message.** Build Rapport. Connect by offering a cutting edge value proposition: expert special counsel "on demand".
4. **Of Counsel Cross-Marketing.** Give them access to your marketing materials and share them with their clientele and other networks.

Your Contemporary Website

Much like your other marketing materials, the quality of your online presence will be a huge factor in the successful growth of your firm. If you do not already have a modern, responsive website, the announcement of your new specialty law services is the ideal opportunity to get one built.

Today's clients are relying heavily on the internet to find legal services. Remember, this is the number one reason specializing is becoming a much more common career choice for lawyers!

An attractive, fully responsive (many of your prospective clients will be searching for you on mobile devices), thoroughly informative and advanced-featured website is **absolutely key in retaining and educating a client** after getting the word out.

If your firm <u>does</u> have an up-to-date website, new content featuring these additional services and partners will not only increase traffic, but attract new demographics and broaden your clientele! This is yet another example of how a network can spur exponential growth for both hosts and specialists.

A PROFESSIONAL WEBSITE CAN MAKE YOUR NEW VENTURE

Let's say a local business is grappling with an IP issue. To find a lawyer in the area, they are going to specifically search for firms that deal with IP. When you advertise as simply a general business firm, you miss making a connection with this company. Once your specialty content has been added to your site, however, these unreachable clients—i.e. inventors, entrepreneurs, artists and other creators that need sole proprietorships or LLCs set up—discover your name.

Ask Your Of Counsel for Content

Here's another bonus: your of counsel firm <u>already has</u> the information you need to add to your website. And they know a lot. In addition to their core level of expert knowledge, they can help you incorporate their own marketing strategy; to essentially replicate their online marketing presence for your website. Ask them to share as much of their web content as possible, whether it be written language, videos, pictures, audio, or any other type of online promotional tools they have created.

The site should also include headshots and bios of the attorneys you (and your clients) will be working with. This kind of transparency will raise your credibility with both old and new clients alike.

Work with your particular of counsel attorneys to decide what materials most exemplify your firm's branding and policies along with client needs and expectations in equal measure.

This content swap serves as a great way to "get to know" your of counsel. You will begin to familiarize yourself with your chosen specialty, and finally, as the content is republished, your partnership is made official.

Notes

Chapter 4

Final Advice

Never underestimate the power of partnerships

Unify forces, share resources and allow the legal profession to flourish.

In short, this is what can be accomplished in a properly maintained of counsel relationship. How? We use our four main goals as guiding principles, of course:

1. **Diversify Revenue Streams**
2. **Serve the Legal System**
3. **Promote Innovation & Business**
4. **Engage in Collective Learning**

To give you a sense of the potential bigger picture and for the sake of trajectory, let's take a brief look at how of counsels and referrals can multiply a network and broaden the reach of our goals.

The Potential Referral Stream

Your firm alone can only have so much of a geographic reach. However, as you solidify your first partnership, you may then begin the process of developing forays into <u>other</u> specialty practice areas.

As you develop these relationships, it becomes clear that bringing on more than one of counsel firm has a remarkable multiplier effect on **the potential referral stream** for all parties involved. This effect then creates a very powerful network.

To be sure, your of counsel firms are now also your advocates in the field. By this point you will have recognized that they have yet another stake in your success: you have, as the host firm, become an expert at managing and bringing on clients.

Conversely, as you add each of counsel firm, <u>you</u> are now connected into <u>their</u> network of clients and referrals.

What you will in effect be doing by reaching out and taking on of counsel partners is build this network, little by little.

The result will be the realization of the four main goals, the importance of which I cannot highlight enough:

1. More Money for all parties
2. Better served, better educated clients means
3. Even more money for all parties and;
4. A growing, powerful network of related firms, which also means
5. More money for all parties

Again, I have extensive first-hand experience as an of counsel attorney with my firm, Bold IP. I have seen for myself the incredible value in working in concert with your colleagues. I have seen infinitely more prosperity in this approach then I have ever witnessed when attorneys operate with a competitive and secretive spirit.

There are of course no shortcuts. For this is true in any field or for any lasting achievement. However, if your ultimate goal is to expand and grow your firm, there is no better way than a committed and considered approach to the of counsel relationship.

❖ ❖ ❖

NOTES

www.ingramcontent.com/pod-product-compliance
Lightning Source LLC
Chambersburg PA
CBHW050028230526
45470CB00003B/1173